The editors would like to thank
BARBARA KIEFER, Ph.D.,
Charlotte S. Huck Professor of Children's Literature,
The Ohio State University, and
LISA KATHLEEN GRADDY,
Deputy Chair and Curator, Division of Political History,
National Museum of American History, Smithsonian Institution,
for their assistance in the preparation of this book.

Visit us on the Web!
Seussville.com
randomhousekids.com

Educators and librarians, for a variety of teaching tools, visit us at RHTeachersLibrarians.com

Library of Congress Cataloging-in-Publication Data
Names: Worth, Bonnie, author. | Ruiz, Aristides, ill. | Mathieu, Joe, ill.
Title: One vote, two votes, I vote, you vote : all about voting / by Bonnie Worth ;
illustrated by Aristides Ruiz and Joe Mathieu.
Description: New York : Random House, 2016. | Series: The Cat in the Hat's learning library
Identifiers: LCCN 2015041949 | ISBN 978-0-399-55598-5 (trade) | ISBN 978-0-399-55599-2 (lib. bdg
ISBN 978-1-5247-1633-2 (pbk.)
Subjects: LCSH: Voting—United States—Juvenile literature. |
Elections—United States—Juvenile literature.
Classification: LCC JK1978 .W67 2016 | DDC 324.6/50973—dc23

Printed in the United States of America   10 9 8 7 6 5 4 3 2 1

One Vote, Two Votes, I Vote, You Vote

by Bonnie Worth

illustrated by Aristides Ruiz and Joe Mathieu

The Cat in the Hat's Learning Library®

Random House 🏠 New York

Voting is something
we do every day.
It's a way we can choose
that gives us our own say.

class trip:
museum

2. zoo

3. beach

ass pet:
gerbil

2. guinea pig

3. goldfish

ass snack:
pple

2. carrot

3. grapes

CLASS ELECTIONS
☑ TODAY ☺

We vote for class president,
and which snack to get,
where to go on class trip,
what to pick as class pet.

7

Voting gives each of us
our very own voice.
It allows a large group
to make ONE single choice.

HOW DO YOU VOTE?

With a proudly raised hand,

marks on paper,

thumbs up or thumbs down—
understand?

Can you choose NOT to vote?
Yes, but that's a sure way
to lose your own voice
and to not have a say.

The item or person
that most of us select
will wind up the winner—
the one we elect.

The biggest of all of America's voting events chooses our president and vice president.

Are presidents important?
Oh, yes, they are—very!
They head up the government
and the military.

Vice presidents take over
on the unhappy day
when presidents get sick
or else pass away.

Every four years,
we elect them, you see,
because we live in
a DEMOCRACY—
a government
FOR the people
and run BY them, too,
which means that
this country
is governed by YOU.

13

Every two years, we elect senators
and congresspeople of our choice
to make laws in Washington
and be our state's voice.

We also elect sheriffs
and mayors and such.
Do local elections count?
You bet, just as much!

MAYER for MAYOR

DRUDGE FOR JUDGE

When our Founders drew up
the Constitution, it's true,
they said folks should vote,
but they did not say *who*.

Since then, our history
is marked by brave fights
waged by people who struggled
to win voting rights
for all of the races
and for all womankind,
and also for eighteen-
year-olds, bear in mind.

VOTING RIGHTS
TIMELINE:

1870

15TH Amendment:
BLACK MEN CAN VOTE.

1920

19TH Amendment:
WOMEN CAN VOTE.

That means that quite soon
you will get to vote, too.
So please pay attention.
This matters to YOU!

1924

1971

CITIZENSHIP ACT:
NATIVE AMERICANS
CAN VOTE.

26TH Amendment:
18-YEAR-OLDS
CAN VOTE.

Only citizens can vote
and, as you've just been told,
people who are at least
eighteen years old.

TOWN HALL

REGISTER

VOTER REGISTRATION

VOTE

REGISTER
HERE TO
VOTE

You must sign up in person
or on the Internet
with name, address, and birth date.
And one more thing yet:

You can write down your party,
if you do not mind.
Cakes and ice cream, you're thinking?
Is the party that kind?

THIS kind of party,
I'm here to report,
is the kind that we know as
the political sort.

It's made up of large
groups of citizens who
share beliefs and ideas
and opinions, too.

Democrats and Republicans
are the biggest two.
Plus small parties to pick from—
more than just a few.

In primary elections
(run before November),
votes will be cast
by each party member
for the candidate who,
they hope and they pray,
will be on the ballot
come Election Day.

SNOW vs. SKINNER

Candidates set out
on the campaign trail
to convince voters
that they will not fail.

"A vote for me,"
the candidates say,
"will make your dreams
come true someday."

With speeches and ads
and town hall meetings,
with handshakes and waves
and cheery greetings,
they work to win
the voters' trust.
To win nomination,
this is a must.

I may be wrong,
but it does seem to me
that voting is one BIG
responsibility!

As a voter, you must
follow news carefully.
You should read, watch, and listen,
and then try to see
what the candidates,
if elected, plan to do.
What are their beliefs?
Do they ring true for you?

Debates are held
for the people to see
the candidates talk
on live TV!

Moderators on hand
have questions to ask.
To give their best answer
is the candidates' task.

1ST NATIONAL DEBATE

A debate is an argument
that's meant to sway.
It is run by rules
in a most formal way.

At meetings called rallies,
supporters get out
to cheer the candidate
they care most about.

Supporters on the phone
or going door-to-door say,
"Vote for my party
on Election Day!"

They raise lots of money,
collect change in jars,
and sell campaign stickers
to stick on cars!

George Washington won the vote,
so I have been told,
during a winter
that was snowy and cold.

In 1845,
Congress passed a vote to say
there would be an earlier
Election Day.

NOVEMBER

The day, each year,
is easy to remember.
It's the Tuesday after the first
Monday in November.

This date was chosen
for a very good reason.
It came at the end of
the harvesting season.

When Election Day comes
the voter's big role
is to make sure to vote
at their assigned poll!

A poll is where you vote.
As a general rule,
it is a public place—
like a firehouse or school.

If you're out of town,
there's a chance that you might
mail an absentee ballot.
Voting is your right!

People cast their votes
by different means—
ballots fed into computers
or direct voting machines.

However you vote,
it's important, you see,
that voters are given
complete privacy!

A curtain or screen
protects voters from view.
This ensures that your vote
is known only to YOU.

VOTING BOOTH

VOTE

The polls close up
at the end of the day.
Here come the counters!
Please clear the way!

VOTE HERE

POLLS CLOSED

BOX 616

BOX 714

BOX 673

By special computer,
poll results are scanned.
But some votes are still
counted out by hand.

The results are sent
to the Board of Elections,
which declares the winner
after careful inspections.

BOX
302

The loser admits their bitter defeat.

The winner announces their victory sweet!

The winner vows to serve everyone in the land—not just the supporters who lent them a hand.

Woo-hoo for THING 2!

If all of this rings true, it is my dearest hope that . . .

you will cast your first vote

for the Cat in the Hat!

VOTE FOR
THE CAT!

GLOSSARY

Absentee: A person who is expected to be somewhere but is not.

Ballot: The act of or process of voting, usually on paper, and in secret.

Campaign: A series of acts intended to achieve a particular goal.

Candidate: A person who applies for a job or is nominated for election.

Citizen: A legally recognized member of a state or country.

Electronic: Referring to a device having computer parts.

Inspection: A close study.

Moderator: A person who directs a debate or discussion.

Nominate: To propose someone to run for office.

Political: Having to do with government affairs.

Poll: The place where voting takes place or the act of voting.

Responsibility: The state of having a duty.

Scan: To read, with the eye or by electronic means.

Sway: To convince or change someone's mind by means o speech or argument.

FOR FURTHER READING

I Could Do That!: Esther Morris Gets Women the Vote by Linda Arms White, illustrated by Nancy Carpenter (Farrar, Straus and Giroux, Melanie Kroupa Books). The story of a spirited young woman who won the vote for women in the Wyoming Territory in 1869. A Bank Street Best Children's Book of the Year. For kindergarten and up.

If I Were President by Catherine Stier, illustrated by DyAnne DiSalvo-Ryan (Albert Whitman & Company). Six children take turns posing as president of the United States in this simple look at the various responsibilities of the president. For kindergarten and up.

Lillian's Right to Vote: A Celebration of the Voting Rights Act of 1965 by Jonah Winter, illustrated by Shane W. Evans (Random House, Schwartz & Wade). As a hundred-year-old African American woman walks up the hill to her polling place, she looks back on her family's history and the history of the fight for voting rights. An author's note includes information about the real woman who inspired Lillian. For kindergarten and up.

Vote! by Eileen Christelow (Clarion Books). This award-winning book about a mayoral election—told in comic-book style—is an accessible and fun introduction to all the steps involved in an election. For grades 1 and up.

INDEX